H. Sandberg

Mammolina

Mammolina

A Story about Maria Montessori

by Barbara O'Connor
illustrations by Sara Campitelli

foreword by Margot R. Waltuch
Association Montessori Internationale

Especially for Mrs. Sandberg's
Room — Best wishes,

Barbara
O'Connor
1998

A Carolrhoda Creative Minds Book

Carolrhoda Books, Inc./Minneapolis

To Willy and Grady, with love—and to Jacqueline, with thanks

This edition of this book is available in two bindings:
Library binding by Carolrhoda Books, Inc.
Soft cover by First Avenue Editions
241 First Avenue North
Minneapolis, Minnesota 55401

Library of Congress Cataloging-in-Publication Data

O'Connor, Barbara.
    Mammolina : a story about Maria Montessori / by Barbara O'Connor ;
with a foreword by Margot Waltuch ; illustrated by Sara Campitelli.
       p.   cm. — (A Carolrhoda creative minds book)
    Includes bibliographical references (p.).
    Summary: Describes the life and achievements of the Italian woman
doctor who developed a revolutionary method of educating children.
    ISBN 0-87614-743-0 (lib. bdg.)
    ISBN 0-87614-602-7 (pbk.)
    1. Montessori, Maria, 1870-1952—Juvenile literature. 2. Educators—
Italy—Biography—Juvenile literature. 3. Montessori method of
education—Juvenile literature. [1. Montessori, Maria, 1870-1952.
2. Educators. 3. Montessori method of education.] I. Campitelli,
Sara, ill. II. Title. III. Series.
LB775.M8026 1993
370'.92—dc20
[B]   92-415
                                                             CIP
                                                              AC

Manufactured in the United States of America

1 2 3 4 5 6 98 97 96 95 94 93

Table of Contents

Foreword 6

School Days 9

Taming the Lions 16

New Direction 24

No Ordinary School 35

Mammolina 50

A Typical Day
  at the Casa dei Bambini 62

Bibliography 64

Foreword

As a student at a Montessori school or just as an interested person, you may wonder who Maria Montessori was. Maria Montessori dedicated her life to the advancement of all children. This book traces her life from her youth, to her struggles as a young adult striving to become the first woman doctor in Italy, to her years as a world figure in education and as an advocate for peace. It also illustrates the independent, imaginative, vital nature that characterized Maria Montessori.

I had the privilege of working closely with Maria Montessori in Laren, Holland, during the period in which she developed the world view that she referred to as "cosmic education." She believed strongly in the notion of the Universal Child—that learning is a total life experience for all children, and that children of every land and culture develop in fundamentally the same way.

Maria Montessori greatly influenced my life and the lives of others with her humor, intelligence, and boundless energy. I hope her story will inspire you to participate in her hope that we can unite for the building of peace, in people and in the world.

MARGOT R. WALTUCH
ASSOCIATION MONTESSORI INTERNATIONALE
REPRESENTATIVE TO THE UNITED NATIONS

① School Days

In a dark, crowded schoolroom in Rome, Italy, a group of girls sat in long rows, sewing silently. Their heads were bowed in concentration. They sat very straight, with their long skirts smoothed neatly over their legs. One of those girls was Maria Montessori.

Maria didn't mind doing needlework. It wasn't as boring as reciting lessons. At least when she was sewing, she could think about more interesting things. Sometimes she tried to imagine what school was like for the boys. In the 1870s, most people thought it wasn't proper for boys and girls to sit together in the same classroom. Were the boys sitting on the same hard benches? Were they reciting the same dull lessons? Was their teacher standing at the front of the room, reading the same words over and over? One thing Maria knew for sure. They were not doing needlework.

As a young child, Maria was not particularly ambitious about schoolwork. She was content to receive awards for *lavori donneschi* (women's work), the needlework she worked at so intently, although she got good grades in all her subjects. Like many girls her age, nine-year-old Maria wanted to be an actress. Rome had many theaters, so Maria thought there must be a lot of acting jobs. She knew that if she didn't become an actress, there was not much else to do except become a teacher. But teachers were stern-faced, bored women who did nothing but read lessons to stern-faced, bored girls. No, she would not like to be a teacher.

On the playground, Maria was usually the leader. She had such an air of authority about her, the other children found themselves naturally following her orders. Sometimes her playmates thought she was bossy and rude. But Maria either didn't notice or didn't care. She was a happy, self-confident child.

Ever since Maria was born, in 1870, Renilde Montessori had hoped her daughter would be able to do things that hadn't been proper for a girl growing up in Renilde's time. Renilde was a bright, well-educated woman who encouraged her daughter to read, ask questions, and study hard. She thought it was important for girls to have a good education. With her mother's influence, Maria began to enjoy her studies more and more.

Renilde was pleased when Maria showed a special interest in mathematics. Perhaps Maria had inherited her talent for working with numbers from her father, Alessandro, who was an accountant. To Maria, reading a math book was just as much fun as playing with dolls. Once she even took a math book to the theater and read during the performance!

By the time she was twelve, Maria was thinking more and more about her future. She would be graduating from primary school soon. For most girls in Italy in the 1800s, primary school was as far as their education went. But Maria began to realize that she didn't want to quit school to become an actress. She wanted to continue her education instead. She knew it wasn't impossible. Some girls went on to secondary school. There was just one problem. Most of them studied literature and languages at the classical school.

Maria wasn't interested in Greek and Latin. She was interested in mathematics, which was taught at the technical school. Very few girls attended technical school, but that didn't bother Maria. She decided she was going to study math. Maria was quite pleased with her decision. Her father, however, was not so pleased. Technical school was for boys, he told her. And math! Why on earth would a girl need to study math? The very idea was appalling!

Maria would not give up easily. She tried to convince him. She argued. Then she begged. But Alessandro would not listen. Maria was heartbroken. Why couldn't he understand? It seemed natural that his only child would share his love of math. But Alessandro had old-fashioned ideas. He was not a man who welcomed change. Young girls needed wit and charm, not math, he thought. And most of Italian society agreed with him.

Luckily Renilde supported Maria's decision to attend technical school without hesitation. Perhaps she saw in Maria the adventurous young girl she herself had always wanted to be. Her daughter was a bit of a rebel—and Renilde loved it. Alessandro was no match for his stubborn wife and daughter. Reluctantly, he gave in.

Maria would enter technical school in the fall of 1883, just after her thirteenth birthday. That summer seemed to last for years. Maria passed the time reading and doing needlework. But mostly she thought about school. What would it be like?

It didn't take long for Maria to discover that going to school with boys was no more interesting than going to school with girls. She enjoyed learning more about history and geography, and she was eager to study new subjects, such as calligraphy and Italian literature. But the classes were always the same. The students sat at their desks for hours, memorizing and repeating rules from a text. Even math, her favorite subject, seemed boring. If only she could ask questions, or try an experiment, or at least move on to the next lesson, learning would be more fun. But Maria was determined to finish school. She did not even consider quitting.

After a few years in technical school, Maria decided to become an engineer. Even though most of the other students planned to be engineers, too, Maria dreaded telling her father. She could just imagine how he would react. "But engineering is for boys!" he would say.

Maria was right. Alessandro was shocked and confused by his daughter's decision. Why couldn't she just be a teacher like other young women?

But by the time she graduated from technical school, in the summer of 1890, Maria had once again changed her mind about her career. She wasn't going to become an engineer after all, she told her father. But before Alessandro had a chance to breathe a sigh of relief, Maria made another announcement. She had decided to become a doctor instead.

Taming the Lions

"Shocking!"

"Unheard of!"

"A woman doctor? Impossible!"

Maria heard the same words over and over—from friends, from family, and of course from her father. No woman in Italy had ever gone to medical school. Alessandro Montessori would have disapproved of any woman attempting something so outrageous. But his own daughter? He would not forbid her to study medicine, he told her, but he could never approve.

Once again, Renilde sided with her daughter. She was delighted at Maria's bold decision. Her husband's angry disapproval didn't bother her a bit. She knew Maria would make a fine doctor.

Maria set out to accomplish her goal with her usual self-confidence. Hoping to win approval for her unusual career choice, she went to visit Dr. Guido Baccelli, head of the medical faculty at the University of Rome. She told him of her plan to attend medical school after earning her undergraduate degree and asked for his support. Dr. Baccelli was appalled at the idea of a woman studying medicine. He said her plan was impossible and flatly refused to offer her any support at all.

Maria was undaunted. Upon parting, she politely shook his hand, thanked him for his time, and announced firmly, "I *know* I shall become a doctor."

Twenty-year-old Maria began her undergraduate studies in science and math at the University of Rome in 1890. She received high marks in all her classes and was awarded her diploma in 1892. She was ready to apply to medical school. Ignoring the overwhelming disapproval she faced, Maria persisted until she was finally accepted. No one is sure how she did it. Maria Montessori was the first woman in all of Italy to study medicine. She knew she faced the biggest challenge of her life. Four long years lay ahead of her. Could she do it? Maria believed she could.

Like all university students, Maria lived at home with her parents. She devoted every minute of the day (and most of the night) to her studies. While other women her age were sewing, practicing piano, and being courted by young men, Maria was studying physics, chemistry, and botany. She never missed a class. One winter when a huge snowstorm struck, Maria plodded through the deep snow in her long skirt to attend class. By the time she arrived, she was soaking wet and cold to the bone. She was also the only student there! The professor who had come to give the lecture was so impressed by her determination to attend class that he gave his lecture anyway.

Although Maria quickly earned the respect of her professors at the university, earning the respect of the other students was much more difficult. Not a day went by that Maria wasn't reminded of the one thing that set her apart from the others: she was a woman. She may have been studying to become a doctor, but she was still expected to obey the social rules of the nineteenth century. Maria had to be escorted to and from school by her disapproving father, because it was not proper for a young lady to walk outdoors alone. Once inside the school building, Maria had to wait until the last student had entered the classroom and taken his seat before she was allowed to go in. It would have been shameful for a woman to come in close contact with men in the hallways.

Sometimes the other students arranged it so there were no seats left by the time Maria came into the classroom. Then Maria would have to stand in the back of the room during the two-hour class. She would hear the snickers of the other students as they enjoyed their mutual joke. But Maria was determined not to let them get the best of her. She responded to them with patience, good humor, and an occasional glare. Once when the student behind her persisted in kicking the back of her chair, Maria gave him such a look that he later told a friend, "I must be immortal or a look like that would have killed me."

Maria Montessori had one goal—to become a doctor. She was not about to let a school full of men stand in her way.

Despite her restrictions, Maria was happy most of the time. But there were also times when she felt discouraged. Her father remained cold and withdrawn. The other students shunned and teased her. And then there was the ordeal of anatomy class, where medical students were required to dissect human bodies. Maria disliked cutting up bodies and handling organs. But to make matters worse, she had to do her dissecting at night—alone. It would not have been proper for a woman to study a body in the company of men.

Maria would never forget her first night in the Institute of Anatomy. It took all her willpower to keep from running out of the room. In the cupboards were the body parts of criminals—intestines in one jar, brains in another. Their skulls were neatly lined up and labeled in black ink: "Murderer," "Thief." In a basin lay bones with pink flesh still clinging to them. In a corner stood an enormous skeleton. "As I stared at it," Maria wrote to a friend, "it seemed to move. I turned my eyes away and began to walk back and forth, repelled by everything I saw."

The terrible smell of the chemicals in the dissecting room made Maria sick. Once she paid a man to stand beside her and smoke cigarettes.

She even tried smoking herself—anything to get rid of the awful odor of the corpses.

Maria began to think she had made the wrong decision when she had chosen medical school. She faced so many obstacles that sometimes she wondered if it was worth it. It would have been much easier just to quit. But Maria was not a quitter. She pushed her doubts aside and continued on with renewed energy. "In those days," she told a friend years later, "I felt as if I could have done anything."

During her last two years in school, Maria studied children's medicine, called pediatrics. She gained practical experience by working at a children's hospital in Rome. She loved the work and was fast becoming an expert on the illnesses of children. She also took a special interest in psychiatry, the medical study of mental illness, and performed research at the psychiatric clinic of the university.

In 1896, after six long years at the university, Maria was finally nearing the end of her studies. At that time, like all medical students, she was required to give a lecture to the entire senior class. She walked out onto the stage and looked down at the auditorium filled with men. She knew many of them were eager to criticize her. She was afraid they might even hoot and jeer. But when she finished her lecture, she was surprised by the sound of applause. Her classmates rose to their feet, shouting, "*Brava!*" (Fine job!) and "*Bene!*" (Good!).

Through teary eyes, Maria saw one figure that stood out from all the rest. In the very last row stood her father. He was clapping! He was smiling! He had accepted her at last. This was a day Maria would never forget. "I felt like a lion tamer that day," she would later recall.

On July 10, 1896, at the age of twenty-five, Maria earned her medical degree and the title of *dottoressa* (female doctor). She had done it! She was the first female doctor in Italy.

A New Direction

Maria was eager to leave university life behind and start the real work of practicing medicine. She wasted no time. Four months after receiving her diploma, young Dottoressa Montessori had three jobs! In addition to working as an assistant at two hospitals, she opened her own clinic. Maria's former university professors began referring patients to her, especially children. They knew Maria was interested in pediatric medicine. Soon the waiting room of Maria's new office was crowded with patients.

Maria was often called away from her office to the home of a sick child. Sometimes after diagnosing and treating her young patient, she would tidy the bedroom, fluff the pillows, and cook a hot bowl of soup. A close friend once described her as "servant, cook, nurse, and doctor in one."

Maria was happy in her new career. She never could have guessed that only one year after her graduation from medical school, her work would lead her in a new direction. But that is exactly what happened.

Despite her busy schedule, Maria managed to continue her research at the psychiatric clinic of the University of Rome. In 1897 she joined the clinic staff as an assistant doctor. Maria wondered how she could possibly take on another job, but she found psychiatry fascinating. Somehow she would find the time and energy.

One of her duties in her new position was to visit asylums, or homes for people with mental illnesses. There she observed the patients and chose those she thought would be suitable for treatment at the clinic. Maria found herself drawn to the children. Some of these children were mentally retarded. Others were emotionally disturbed or had severe behavior problems. In the asylums, they were kept like prisoners, in bare, dark rooms. They had nothing to play with. They had nothing to do but sleep and eat.

Maria was troubled by the children she saw.

She thought about them constantly. Surely there was a way to help them. And she knew asylums weren't the answer.

During a visit to one of the asylums, Maria was told how after meals the children would crawl around on the floor, looking for the crumbs of bread that had dropped there. Maria listened but made no reply. She watched the children. She looked at the bare walls of the empty room. Suddenly a new idea occurred to her. Maybe these children weren't grabbing for crumbs because they were hungry. Maybe they just needed something to look at or touch. The bread crumbs were their only toys.

The longer Maria studied the children, the more she became convinced that they could be helped. What if they were given some activity to do? How would they respond if they had objects to hold, colors to look at, shapes to feel?

Maria loved solving problems, and she was determined to solve the problem of the children of the asylums. She began to read everything she could find about retarded and emotionally disturbed children. She read about methods of treatment that had been used in the past. And she continued to watch the children, making notes about her observations and ideas.

Finally Maria came to a conclusion that would change the course of her life forever. These children belonged in schools, not hospitals, she decided. These children were special, and they needed special schools. Maria decided she would learn everything she could about the education of young children. Then she would think of a way to help the children of the asylums.

Each night, after a long day treating patients in her office and at the hospitals, Maria went home to study. She was certain she was on the right track. Finally she made a plan—a plan for a school for children with special needs.

The classroom of Maria's school would be filled with objects to touch and hold. There would be a garden full of flowers to see and smell. The children would run and tumble in gymnastics classes. They would even learn the alphabet—not by memorizing letters in a book, but by touching and tracing letters with their fingers. Maria believed that children should learn first with their senses—seeing, feeling, hearing, smelling—then with their minds.

But Maria knew that ideas on paper were not enough. If she was ever going to see her school become a reality, she had to convince others she was right. Maria spent the next two years trying to do just that. She talked to doctors, to teachers, to social workers. She wrote about her ideas in magazines and medical journals. She gave lectures about her research—first in Rome and then throughout all of Italy.

Maria worked from morning until night. With such a busy schedule, she had little social life. Her closest friends were her colleagues. Maria was especially fond of Dr. Giuseppe Montesano, another assistant doctor at the psychiatric clinic. The two young doctors had much in common and soon became good friends. Maria was glad to have a friend like Giuseppe. He understood her and shared her dreams. It didn't take long for the two friends to fall in love.

In March of 1898, Maria gave birth to Giuseppe's son. But she and Giuseppe did not get married. To this day, no one is certain why.

Maria named her son Mario Montessori. His birth was a secret she and Giuseppe would carry with them for the rest of their lives. Only their parents and closest friends knew the truth. In those days, it was scandalous to have a child without being married. If the truth had been known, Maria's career would have been ruined, putting an end to everything she had worked for.

Sadly Maria accepted the fact that she could not keep her son with her. But she knew she could never give him up completely, either. So little Mario was sent away to live with a family in the countryside near Rome. If she couldn't have him with her, Maria decided, at least she would have him near her. Throughout his childhood, Mario was never told the truth about his real mother. He knew Maria only as the "beautiful lady" who came to visit.

During the fall of 1898, Maria continued to give lectures and write articles about teaching children with special needs. In January 1899, the Italian minister of education invited Maria to give a series of lectures at the teacher-training school in Rome, Collegio Romano. The invitation meant a great deal to Maria. Of course she was excited about the chance to discuss her research with the future teachers of Italy. But she had another reason to be happy about this invitation. The minister of education was Dr. Guido Baccelli, the same man who had refused to support her decision to apply to medical school eight years before!

In the spring of 1900, Maria got some wonderful

news. A new school was opening in Rome—a school to train teachers to work with children who had mental and emotional problems. The teachers would work with twenty-two children who would attend school there. Maria was asked to be one of the two directors needed to run the school. The other director was to be Giuseppe Montesano. Maria was thrilled. Now she would have a chance to try out her ideas with the children. She never could have imagined such a perfect job!

Not yet thirty years old, Maria worked at her new job with her usual energy and determination. Her natural curiosity and love of challenge had led her into teaching—the very career she had always said she would not want!

But Maria was no ordinary teacher. She was with the children all day—teaching, watching, experimenting. At night, Maria made notes about what she had observed during the day. Then she made sketches and models of teaching materials. When she thought a design was right, she had the materials manufactured. Before long Maria's classroom was filled with shapes to hold, beads to thread, laces to tie. There were objects of different sizes, colors, and textures to match and sort. There were things to feel, to smell, to listen to.

One of Maria's designs was a three-dimensional wooden alphabet. She painted the vowels red and the consonants blue. She gave the alphabet to the children and sat back to watch. Maria was fascinated when the children touched the letters over and over.

Then one day Maria's heart nearly burst with joy. The children began writing letters with chalk on the blackboard! The children that society had given up on had taught themselves to write.

Now the children were ready to learn the sounds of the letters. Day after day Maria worked with them, pointing and naming, pointing and naming. "This is i." "This is o." Eventually the children were able to identify a letter by its sound. "Looking becomes reading; touching becomes writing," Maria wrote, describing her unusual method. Some of the children made so much progress that Maria took them to a public school to take a reading and writing test with normal children. They passed the test. Maria had known her methods would work, and she had proved it.

But Maria was still not completely satisfied. She couldn't help wondering what would happen if the same methods were used to teach children who were not mentally retarded. If retarded children could make this much progress, what would normal children do? Would they learn more quickly than children taught the traditional way?

Maria had something new to think about.

4

No Ordinary School

Despite Maria's success at the school, she unexpectedly quit her job in 1901. Her friends were puzzled. She was making such progress with the children. Why was she quitting now? they wondered.

But Maria would not explain. Perhaps she left because her relationship with Giuseppe had ended and he had married someone else.

Whatever her reasons, Maria put Giuseppe and the school behind her and looked toward the future. Where should she go from here? She thought a lot about the work she had done at the school. She was amazed at how much the children had learned—and how quickly they had learned it. But she still couldn't help wondering what would happen if she used the same methods to teach normal children.

Once again Maria's curiosity led her in a new direction. In the five years since her graduation from medical school, she had become a well-known authority on teaching children with special needs. But now she wanted to know more about the education of normal children. "Little by little," Maria later said, "I became convinced that similar methods applied to normal children would develop or set free their personality in a marvelous and surprising way."

Now thirty years old, Maria returned to the University of Rome. She took courses that would help her learn more about how children learn—philosophy, psychology, and anthropology—as well as some courses on teaching and hygiene. She studied the work of other experts in the field of special education. She also visited elementary schools to observe teachers and students. She was surprised at how little had changed since her own school days. Children still recited their lessons in unison. They sat stiffly in the same neat rows, "like butterflies mounted on pins." She could almost see herself sitting there among them.

By 1904 Maria's studies and observations had convinced her that the time had come for the schools of Italy to change. Everything she had learned seemed to confirm a thought that had been gnawing at her for a long time: children should not be forced to learn. They *want* to learn. With the right materials and the right environment, Maria believed, they would choose to learn.

Although she was still practicing medicine at her office and in several hospitals in Rome, Maria managed to find time to begin her campaign to reform the schools of Italy. She published articles about her research in magazines. She taught a course for teachers at the University of Rome. She lectured at teachers' conferences.

Maria was a talented public speaker. She never used notes, but she spoke with poise and confidence, waving her arms or shaking a fist to make a point. She was witty, and most of all, she was convincing. Her audience believed in her.

Maria enjoyed reading, writing, and talking about education. But more than anything, she wanted to work with children. She knew that only by working with children would she ever really know if she was right.

Her chance came in 1906. That year a group of wealthy bankers came to Maria with an interesting offer. They told her about an apartment building they had renovated to provide cheap housing for the city's poor and homeless. The tenement was located in the San Lorenzo district of Rome.

This area was known for its poverty and slums. Most of the building's tenants were poor working parents of young children. The children who were not old enough to go to school were simply left home alone while their parents went to work. With no one to supervise them, the children were free to run and play throughout the building. They scribbled on the newly painted walls and scattered trash around the halls.

To keep the children from ruining the building, the bankers decided to provide a room for them to stay in during the day. But they needed someone to keep the children occupied and out of mischief. The bankers had heard about Maria's work and thought she might be just the person they were looking for.

Maria had been waiting for just such a challenge. She would take the job on one condition: she wanted to have complete control over how the children's room was run. The bankers agreed.

Maria decided to name her little school Casa dei Bambini, which means "Children's House" in Italian. On January 6, 1907, Casa dei Bambini opened its doors. Maria felt as though her life's work was just beginning. She would later recall that she had had a "vision" that this work would prove to be very important. In the speech she gave at the school's official opening, she predicted that someday people would come from all over the world to see her school. Only a woman with the self-confidence of Maria Montessori could have looked at that one empty room and those fifty unruly little children and seen such a promising future.

Maria wanted to spend every hour of the day at her Casa dei Bambini. But besides being the director of the Casa, Maria was still a doctor, teacher, lecturer, and researcher. With the bankers' approval, she hired a teacher to take charge of the classroom so that she would have time to observe and experiment. Right away she brought in some of the teaching materials she had designed. Maria called them "sensory materials," because she believed they helped sharpen a child's senses. Some of them were new, and others were modified versions of materials used with the retarded and disturbed children.

The teacher at the Casa must have been puzzled when Maria gave her the materials and then instructed her to leave the children alone with them. "I merely wanted to study the children's reactions," Maria later explained. "I asked her not to interfere with them in any way as otherwise I would not be able to observe them."

Maria was pleased when the children ignored the dolls and wagons and went right for the cylinders, cubes, rods, and other wooden shapes she had designed. Sometimes hours would slip by as she watched the children. She was always thinking of new things to try. Often she could hardly wait to get to school with some new design she had worked on the night before. She liked to see which objects the children preferred and how they used them. She was fascinated when they figured out for themselves how to place cylinders in the right holes or how to arrange cubes in order of size to build a tower. They didn't need the teacher to show them how to fit circles, squares, and triangles into matching spaces on a board.

Maria was surprised at how even the three- and four-year-olds worked with total concentration, often repeating a task over and over again. She also noticed that the children learned some skills more easily at certain ages. Once the children had passed that age, it took them longer to learn the skill. She called these stages "sensitive periods" for learning. The more she observed, the more she realized how important it was to let the children choose their own materials. They seemed to have a natural instinct for their own sensitive periods. A whole library full of books and a lifetime at a university could never have taught Maria what she learned from watching the children.

Maria could not be at the school every day, but she came as often as her busy schedule allowed. The little children of the Casa loved having her visit. As soon as she walked in the door, they ran to greet her. They liked this plump lady with the calm smile. Now in her late thirties, Maria dressed in dark, stylish dresses and wore her dark brown hair arranged neatly on top of her head. The children never seemed to mind her watching them so closely. They liked it when she wandered over to talk to them or ask a question. She made them feel important because she was always interested in what they had to say.

As the weeks passed, Maria continued to make changes to the Casa dei Bambini. She designed child-size tables and chairs that were light enough for the children to move by themselves. She had little sinks put in so they could wash themselves. She took out the locked cupboards and replaced them with open shelves low enough for the children to reach.

Almost everything about the Casa dei Bambini set it apart from ordinary schools. Sunny windowsills were lined with plants and flowers. Tabletops now held rabbit cages or fishbowls. The children moved freely around the room, choosing whatever materials interested them. They worked at their tasks for as long as they liked, then put the materials back in the proper place on the shelf. On sunny days, they planted seeds or hoed weeds in the little garden in the courtyard. Best of all, the children were learning and having fun at the same time.

Every child from the youngest to the oldest had jobs to do. They were taught to take care of the plants and animals, prepare and serve their own lunches, and tidy the classrooms. Maria called these housekeeping chores "exercises of practical life." She believed that children should be taught to do things for themselves at an early age. "No one can be free unless he is independent," she often said. What better model of independence could the children have had than Maria Montessori herself!

Sometimes as she watched the children, Maria thought how different her Casa was from that dreary little schoolroom where she had been made to sit all day. These children were not reciting rules about squares and triangles like parrots in a cage. They were holding the shapes, counting the sides, feeling the corners.

Maria was pleased with the way her school was developing. She had done far more than merely keep the children from running wild. Evidently the building owners also were pleased. They asked Maria to organize a school in one of the other tenements, too. On April 7, 1907, only three months after the first school had opened, the second Casa dei Bambini was opened in San Lorenzo.

That fall Maria decided to try another experiment. In those days, children were never taught to read or write until they were six. Preschool children, most people believed, were too young to learn such skills. Maria was not so sure she agreed. She had used special methods to teach the children from the asylums to write. Maybe her preschoolers could learn by similar methods.

Late in the afternoon after all the children had gone home, Maria and her assistants would gather in one of the empty classrooms. They sat on the little chairs in their long skirts, cutting letters of the alphabet out of cardboard and sandpaper and gluing them together.

Maria put the letters in an old cardboard case and placed the case on a shelf in one of the classrooms. The children loved their new "toys." Over and over again, they held, traced, felt, and sorted the letters. Next the children learned to make the sound of each letter. For weeks they practiced tracing the sandpaper letters with their fingers while making the sound of the letter.

One unusually warm December day, Maria sat outside on the rooftop terrace with the children. A five-year-old boy sat beside her. He seemed to have nothing to do. Maria gave him a piece of chalk. "Draw me a picture of this chimney," she said to him, pointing to the chimney of the tenement building.

The little boy smiled up at her, eager to show her how well he could draw. He drew a few pictures, then looked up at Maria. "I know how to write!" he told her excitedly as he began writing words on the pavement. Maria jumped up and ran over to him. Yes, he was writing—not just letters, but whole words—*"mano"* (hand), *"camino"* (chimney), *"tetto"* (roof)! Soon the other children gathered around. "Give me the chalk. I can write, too," said one.

As more and more children gathered, the excitement grew. Soon they were writing everywhere—on the pavement, on the shutters, on the doors. Maria described that day as an "explosion into writing," an expression she would use from that day on.

That night Maria got out her cardboard and scissors again. This time she made little signs: *"bambola"* (doll), *"palla"* (ball), *"sedia"* (chair). The next day, almost every object in the Casa was labeled. The children already knew the sounds of the letters. By combining the sounds into syllables, they were able to connect the written word with the object. The children were so excited by their new discovery that they raced around the room, trying to read all the signs.

One day Maria made up a game. One by one, the children were to pick a card out of a basket. If they could read the name of the toy written on the card, they could play with that toy as long as they wanted. But the children didn't want to play with the toys. They just wanted to read the cards!

Maria would never forget the feeling of satisfaction she had that day. "As I stood in meditation among the eager children," she later recalled, "the discovery that it was knowledge they loved, and not the silly game, filled me with wonder."

The four- and five-year-old children of the slums had learned to read and write. If Maria had never done another thing, the world would still remember her for that. But Maria Montessori had just begun.

Mammolina

News of the unusual experiment taking place in San Lorenzo began to spread. Newspapers reported that "miracles" were taking place in Maria's schools. Less than a year after the first Casa opened its doors, journalists, teachers, social workers, and doctors were coming to see for themselves what all the fuss was about.

Maria welcomed these visitors to her schools. She liked to talk to them about her work. It didn't bother her a bit if they doubted what she told them. She knew all they had to do was watch the children. Her visitors may have come to San Lorenzo shaking their heads in doubt, but they left nodding in agreement. The *dottoressa* was, indeed, doing some remarkable things.

One day a man visiting the school was watching a small boy writing on a chalkboard. He was amazed at the skill of such a small child. "Who taught you to write?" the man asked the child.

The little boy looked up from his work with a puzzled expression. "Who taught me?" the boy replied. "Nobody taught me. I learned."

Maria was delighted. "The real teachers of the Montessori method are the children themselves," she had explained so many times. This little boy was all the proof she needed.

Many of the teachers who came to visit the school found themselves returning often. These women were intrigued by the work Maria was doing there and came away with fresh ideas. But professional curiosity was not the only reason for coming back. They liked Maria, too. Besides being intelligent and interesting, she was warm, patient, and motherly. She was just as likely to invite them in to talk about their problems over a plate of pasta and a cup of tea as to lead them in a lively discussion about the role of the teacher in the classroom.

Maria had accomplished many things in her lifetime, but she had never had time to develop lasting friendships. Now, at thirty-eight, she welcomed the companionship of the women who visited her regularly and was flattered by their eagerness to learn about her methods. She became teacher, counselor, friend, and mother to them. They affectionately called her "Mammolina," Italian for "darling mama."

One of these women was Anna Maccheroni. Anna had attended one of Maria's lectures at the University of Rome. At the time, she had been undecided about becoming a teacher, but Maria had inspired her. Now she came to Maria's school often. She saw in Maria not only a brilliant teacher, but a kind and gentle woman. Anna took on more and more responsibilities at the school and eventually became Maria's assistant. Maria had found her match in the energetic and hard-working young woman. Every day the two of them worked until long after the last child had gone home. Then they locked up for the night and headed for Maria's apartment, where she lived with her parents. They sat for hours by a warm fire, talking about the children, the teaching materials, education, or important social issues. Maria's mother, Renilde, was still very interested in her daughter's work and loved to join in their conversations.

With Anna's help, Maria was able to spend less time at her schools and more time recording her research and giving lectures. Many of those who heard her speak were interested in starting schools of their own using Maria's methods and materials. In the fall of 1908, Maria opened three more schools, two in Rome and one in Milan, about three hundred miles away. Less than two years after the children of San Lorenzo had walked through the doors of the first Casa, the name Montessori was known throughout Italy.

In the summer of 1909, Maria did something she hadn't done in a long time: she took a vacation. She had been invited to spend some time relaxing at the elegant villa of a rich baroness. But Maria soon found she was not very good at being idle. For some time, her friends had been urging her to write down her methods. So for lack of anything else to keep her busy, Maria sat on the terrace overlooking the mountains and began to write.

Once she put pen to paper, the words tumbled out so fast that within a month she had completed a book. *The Montessori Method* was published that same year. Within three years, the book was translated into more than twenty languages. At last the Montessori method of teaching had traveled beyond the borders of Italy.

During the next three years, schools based on the Montessori method opened all over the world, from China to Australia to Canada. By the end of 1911, Italy and Switzerland had adopted the Montessori system for all public schools. The first Montessori school in the United States opened in Tarrytown, New York, that same year. Two years later, there were nearly one hundred Montessori schools in the U.S.

Maria was glad to see so many Montessori schools opening. But she worried that her methods and materials might not be used properly. Because a Montessori classroom was so different from a traditional classroom, Maria realized that teachers needed special training. Over the last few years, Maria had spent very little time practicing medicine. Now, at the age of forty, she decided to remove her name from the list of practicing doctors in Italy. She wanted to be able to devote all her time to training teachers and overseeing the opening of schools.

With the help of Anna and her devoted group of followers, Maria began planning her first international teacher-training course. Sadly, her plans were interrupted by the death of her mother five days before Christmas in 1912. Renilde Montessori had been Maria's most avid fan, supporter, confidante, and friend. Maria would miss her terribly. She dressed in black for many years afterward.

Staying busy helped Maria get over the grief of her mother's death. She proceeded with her plans for the teacher training course, which opened in Rome in January 1913. Eighty-seven teachers came from all parts of the world. Maria spoke to the group from a raised platform she shared with a translator. She was a dignified woman of forty-two. Her wavy hair, now streaked with gray, framed a smooth face and sparkling brown eyes. She spoke slowly in Italian, carefully pausing after each sentence to allow time for her words to be translated into English. Her friends sat in the back of the room, proudly watching their Mammolina.

The training course was a tremendous success.

The teachers went home armed with a new way to teach and renewed enthusiasm for their chosen profession. And Maria felt better knowing these teachers would go back to their schools and teach her methods properly. Finally she was seeing her vision of a new kind of school become a reality.

But there was one thing standing in the way of complete happiness for Maria—the absence of her son, Mario. Fifteen years had passed since his birth. Many things had changed in Italy—but one thing had not. The birth of a child to an unwed mother was still a scandal.

Even though Mario had never been told the truth about Maria, he had always known she was someone special. On a warm spring day in 1913, while on a school outing, Mario saw the "beautiful lady" getting out of her car nearby. Years later he would still recall how he went up to her and said, "I know you are my mother." When he told her he wanted to go with her, Maria did not refuse. From that day on, mother and son were always together. She was never able to admit publicly that he was her son, but at least she had him with her.

Following the success of her first international training course, Maria traveled all over the world training teachers, lecturing, and helping teachers establish new schools. Mario went with her on most of her travels. Eventually he became her secretary and assistant. Even after he married and had children of his own, he continued to work with Maria. In 1929 they founded the Association Montessori Internationale to oversee the Montessori schools and supervise the training of teachers.

Maria devoted the rest of her life to her work. Over forty years after she opened the first Casa dei Bambini, Maria was still teaching her methods with the same enthusiasm and energy. Even in her later years, it was not unusual for her to fly from Holland to London, have lunch, then fly on to India to give a lecture—all in the same day! But no matter how busy she was, Maria always found time to visit children. As soon as she arrived in a new city, she would ask to be taken to the nearest Montessori school. There she would sit patiently while the children gathered excitedly around their visitor.

"Look at this!"

"Watch me!"

"I can count!"

"Listen to this!"

The little children were always eager to show

Maria what they could do—and Maria was always eager to see.

By 1949 Maria had lived through two World Wars, and she spoke often of her hopes for lasting world peace. "We cannot achieve world harmony simply by attempting to unite all these adult people who are so different," she said, "but we can achieve it if we begin with the child who is not born with racial prejudices." For her lifetime of commitment to the education of children, Maria was nominated for the Nobel Peace Prize in 1949, 1950, and 1951. She was deeply moved by this honor.

On May 6, 1952, while visiting friends in Holland, Maria Montessori died. She was buried in Holland. It had been her wish to be buried wherever she died. The following words are written on a stone at her parents' grave in Italy: Maria Montessori "rests far from her beloved country, far from her dear ones buried here, at her wish as testimony to the universality of the work which made her a citizen of the world."

In her will, Maria left all her possessions to *"il mio figlio"*—"my son." At last, after death, she was able to call Mario her son. At her request, Mario continued the work that she had begun "for the good of mankind."

Maria's ideas did not die with her. Schools everywhere have been influenced in some way by her work. The thousands of Montessori schools all over the world are a tribute to the woman who had a vision—and made it happen.

A Typical Day
at the Casa dei Bambini

9:00-10:00   Arrival and preparation for the day: inspection for cleanliness, help in putting on aprons, exercises of practical life. Discussion of events of the day before. Religious exercises.

10:00-11:00   Intellectual exercises (using sensory materials) and naming lessons (learning the proper words to describe objects, such as "long" and "short," "thick" and "thin"), interrupted by short rest periods.

11:00-11:30   Simple gymnastics: ordinary movements done gracefully, marching in line, lessons in courtesy, placing of objects gracefully

11:30-12:00   Short prayer, lunch

12:00-1:00	Free games
1:00-2:00	Directed games, outside if possible. Older children perform exercises of practical life. All inspected for cleanliness. Discussion.
2:00-3:00	Manual work: clay modeling, design, etc.
3:00-4:00	Gymnastics and songs, outside if possible. Exercises to develop forethought: caring for plants and animals.

Bibliography

Kramer, Rita. *Maria Montessori: A Biography.* Reading, Massachusetts: Addison-Wesley, 1988.

Montessori, Maria. *The Montessori Method.* New York: Schocken, 1964.

Pollard, Michael. *Maria Montessori.* Harrisburg, Pennsylvania: Morehouse, 1990.

Standing, E.M. *Maria Montessori: Her Life and Work.* New York: New American Library, 1957.

Wolf, Aline D. *A Parents' Guide to the Montessori Classroom.* Altoona, Pennsylvania: Parent-Child Press, 1980.